Reading *in Style*

Differentiated Reading Activities for Fiction, Nonfiction, and Poetry

SECOND EDITION

Joyce W. Jackson · Susan C. Morris · Kristen M. Perini

*Reading in Style: Differentiated Reading Activities for Fiction, Nonfiction, and Poetry
(Elementary, Second Edition)*
Joyce W. Jackson, Susan C. Morris, and Kristen M. Perini

Published by Thoughtful Education Press/Silver Strong & Associates LLC
227 First Street, Ho-Ho-Kus, NJ 07423
Phone: 800-962-4432 | Fax: 201-652-1127 | www.ThoughtfulClassroom.com

ISBN # 978-1-58284-044-4

For information, contact:
Permissions Department
Thoughtful Education Press
227 First Street, Ho-Ho-Kus, NJ 07423
Phone: 800-962-4432
Fax: 201-652-1127
Email: questions@ThoughtfulClassroom.com
Website: www.ThoughtfulClassroom.com

President: Harvey F. Silver
Director of Publishing: Matthew J. Perini
Production Editor: Justin M. Gilbert
Design and Production Directors: Bethann Carbone & Michael Heil

Quantity discounts are available. For more information call 800-962-4432.

Printed in the United States of America

ELEMENTARY

Reading *in Style*

Differentiated Reading Activities for Fiction, Nonfiction, and Poetry

SECOND EDITION

CONTENTS

ACKNOWLEDGMENTS

This book is a celebration of reading and the important role it plays in the academic and personal development of our young students. We are thankful to have been supported and guided by so many educators as we developed *Reading in Style*. We would like to take this opportunity to recognize and thank some of the many individuals who have helped us bring this book to you.

First and foremost, we acknowledge the profound and positive impact Dr. Harvey Silver and the late Richard Strong have had on us and this book. Their model of four learning styles and their Task Rotation strategy serve as the foundation of this text.

Sherry Grazda's passionate commitment to using reading styles in her classroom have helped us shape many of the student activities presented in this book. In addition, Jocelyn Thomas and Roberta Panjwani have provided us with new perspectives on our Task Rotations and their use with young readers.

Finally, we want to thank Justin Gilbert for his editorial insight and assistance in managing this book from draft to publication.

ABOUT THE AUTHORS

 **Joyce W. Jackson** is a seasoned teacher with over 30 years of experience in the classroom. She is a trusted consultant in the areas of curriculum design, closing the achievement gap, and school improvement. Before working with teachers as a Silver Strong & Associates coach and mentor, she worked with the Kentucky Department of Education to serve and assist at-risk populations of students.

 **Susan C. Morris**, a former classroom teacher, has over two decades of experience developing practical applications for teachers, students, and parents in the areas of learning styles, multiple intelligences, brain-based research, experiential learning, and curriculum design. As a consultant and coach, she uses a train-the-trainer approach to foster sustainable professional development and incorporates technology to enhance and promote continuous professional learning.

 **Kristen M. Perini** taught fifth grade for seven years in Teaneck, New Jersey. Kristen served as a mentor to new teachers and led her school's professional development initiatives on teacher effectiveness and classroom management. She continues her work in education as a researcher and tutor.

Introduction to **Reading** *Styles*

(Plus a Few Activities)

by Matthew J. Perini

A NOTE ABOUT
CLASSROOM CONNECTIONS

Throughout this introduction, you'll be asked to
think about your own reading preferences and
styles. These activities are marked by a Classroom
Connection icon (as seen at right). Whenever one
of these icons appears, it means that a similar
and more student-friendly version of the activity
is available in the Classroom Connections section,
which begins on page 23. These Classroom
Connections are also available for download
at our online Reading Style Resource Center at
www.ThoughtfulClassroom.com/ReadingResources.

INTRODUCTION TO READING STYLES
(Plus a Few Activities)

How would you characterize yourself as a reader? Do you have any reading rituals? Can you read anywhere, or do you have a special place or a special chair or a special desk just for reading? Does the time of day matter to you? Do you find that you read better in the morning, the afternoon, or the evening? Perhaps you're a night owl and look forward to the pleasure of reading while the raccoons and bats are prowling but the rest of the world has gone to sleep. What about background noise? Are you able to filter out the noise while reading, or do you require absolute silence?

Use the space below to list any reading rituals you have.

ACTIVITY

My Reading Rituals...

CLASSROOM CONNECTION

Here's another way to think about who you are as a reader. Imagine you're stepping foot into a brand new bookstore across town. As you enter, you're hit by an exhilarating blend of scents—the paper-and-ink of books, the oak from the shelves and display tables, swirls of coffee and cinnamon from the café in the corner. As your mind stirs to life, you think to yourself, *If thought had a smell, this would be it*. In front of you are 20,000 square feet of pure joy—the wide world of novels, biographies, cookbooks, travel guides, poetry, self-help, history, romance, science fiction, children's literature, drama, humor, sports writing, the list goes on and on. How do you get around this place? Where's the directory? That's when you look up and see the largest and most unusual bookstore directory you've ever seen.

Figure 1: Bookstore Directory

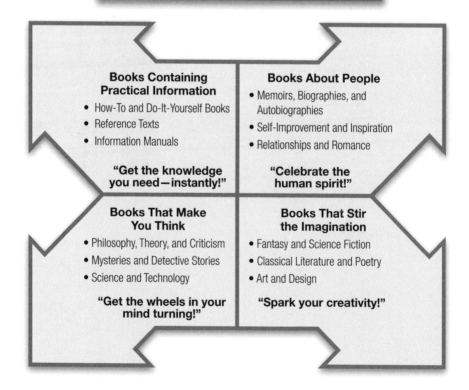

ACTIVITY

CLASSROOM CONNECTION

So, which way do you go?

Which path would you likely avoid?

What might your choices say about you as a reader?

The truth is, no matter how you look at it, reading is a deeply personal act. What's troubling is that many reading programs being implemented in schools across the country fail to take the personal aspects of reading into account. "Here's a list of skills that all readers need," they tell us. It's not that they're wrong. After all, we know that students who know how to find main ideas, summarize, create mental images, manage new vocabulary words, make inferences, and monitor their own comprehension will read with far greater proficiency than students who lack these skills. Rather, the problem lies in the narrow scope of these reading programs: by focusing almost completely on skills, they tend to neglect the fact that all readers have interests, ideas, and ways of thinking that they bring to the reading experience.

In this book, you will explore a simple framework that will allow you to differentiate and personalize reading instruction while you work to build the critical literacy and thinking skills emphasized in the new Common Core State Standards.

This framework

- Will help you respond to the challenge of addressing the Common Core State Standards with engaging activities that students enjoy.

- Accommodates the needs and talents of all readers, not just your best readers.

- Challenges all students to grow as readers and thinkers.

- Is based on more than 35 years of research and practice in thousands of schools across the country.

- Combines the insights of the two most powerful models for understanding cognitive differences—learning styles and multiple intelligences.

- Will bring balance to any reading program by reinforcing the idea that reading is more than just a list of skills to be mastered.

But before you dive headlong into the application of this framework in the classroom, we need to take a little detour. When we finish this detour, you will know (almost) everything you need to know about this framework, including how it works and why it matters. The purpose of this detour is to introduce you to the central concept of this book: ***reading styles***.

Let's begin our detour by going back to our imaginary bookstore. Imagine that you've skimmed the racks and tables of the section you chose and have found a book that's perfect for you. Here's the question: How are you going to read it? Are you more likely to hunt down specific pieces of information or let your mind savor the words, images, and interesting turns of phrase it finds while reading? Are you more likely to argue with the author and her ideas, or personalize them by connecting them to your own experiences?

In the box below you'll find twelve distinct reading behaviors, or ways of reading. All readers engage in all twelve of these behaviors depending on what they're reading and why they're reading it. You already know what you're reading—your ideal book, which you've located in our imaginary bookstore. You also know why you're reading it—entirely for your own enjoyment. So the question remains: How are you going to read your book? Rank the twelve behaviors in the box below from 1 to 12. A rank of 1 indicates that this is the behavior you're most likely to engage in as you read, while a rank of 12 indicates the behavior you're least likely to engage in.

ACTIVITY

CLASSROOM CONNECTION

Rank these reading behaviors from 1 to 12.
When I read, I...

- [ ] Hunt down specific information.
- [ ] Focus on the important details.
- [ ] Stop and test myself to make sure I remember what I've read.

- [ ] Identify with characters and their problems.
- [ ] Try to make connections between what I'm reading and my own experiences.
- [ ] Talk to someone about the text.

- [ ] Make sure I understand the big ideas.
- [ ] Argue with the author in my head.
- [ ] Figure out if there's any hidden meaning or "subtext" in the reading.

- [ ] Look for interesting words and surprising turns of phrase.
- [ ] Make a picture or movie of the text in my head.
- [ ] Predict what will happen next.

Take a look at your rankings. Are your rankings scattered, or can you find a pattern? For example, does one box have two or three low numbers in it while another box has two or three high numbers in it? If so, this may be an initial indication of your dominant reading style.

Where Do Reading Styles Come From?

The idea behind reading styles can be traced all the way back to one of the founders of modern psychology, Carl Jung. Jung (1923) discovered that the way we acquire new information and evaluate the importance of that information has a huge impact on who we are and the personality we develop. Later, Isabel Myers and Katharine Briggs (Myers, 1962; Myers, et al., 1998) expanded on Jung's work to develop a comprehensive framework for understanding human differences. The result of Myers and Briggs' work is the world-famous Myers-Briggs Type Indicator, which some two million people take every year to help them realize their potential and grow as learners, workers, and citizens. More recently, educational researchers—including Bernice McCarthy (1982), Carolyn Mamchur (1996), Edward Pajak (2003), Harvey Silver and Richard Strong (2004), Gayle Gregory (2005), Jane Kise (2007), and Diane Payne and Sondra VanSant (2009)—have explored the implications of these ideas and applied them specifically to education. In synthesizing this work with our 35 years of experience in helping schools develop all students' literacy skills, we have been able to identify four distinct styles of readers, which are outlined on the following page (see Figure 2).

It is important to note that whenever we talk about reading styles, we are talking about a framework, a way of making distinct reading tendencies noticeable. We are never talking about pigeonholes. No reader is a perfect Mastery reader or Interpersonal reader, or any other style for that matter. We all rely on all four styles to address the challenges posed by different texts. But it is equally true that most readers develop familiarity and strength in one or two styles and tend to be weaker in one or two other styles.

For example, Figures 3 and 4 (pp. 10-11) show two different students' responses to the "Who Am I as a Reader?" student survey, which is included in this book. Take a look at both students' responses. Which styles do you think are prominent in each student's work?

Figure 2: Four Styles of Readers

CLASSROOM CONNECTION

Mastery Readers...

- *Read because* they want to learn practical information.
- *Like texts that* are clear, to the point, and have useful applications.
- *Like reading questions that ask* them to recall information.
- *Experience difficulty when* texts become too poetic or fantasy-oriented.

Interpersonal Readers...

- *Read because* they want to understand themselves and other people.
- *Like texts that* focus on feelings, relationships, and human stories.
- *Like reading questions that ask* them how they feel or what they would do in a given situation.
- *Experience difficulty when* texts become too abstract or complicated.

Understanding Readers...

- *Read because* they want to be challenged to think.
- *Like texts that* contain provocative ideas and controversial issues.
- *Like reading questions that ask* them to explain, prove, or take a position.
- *Experience difficulty when* texts focus heavily on feelings.

Self-Expressive Readers...

- *Read because* they want to use their imagination.
- *Like texts that* are poetic, fantasy-oriented, and stylistically creative.
- *Like reading questions that ask* them to speculate, imagine, and ask "What if?"
- *Experience difficulty when* texts are loaded with details.

Source: Adapted from *Reading for Academic Success, Grades 2-6: Differentiated Strategies for Struggling, Average, and Advanced Readers* (p. 214), by R. W. Strong, H. F. Silver, and M. J. Perini, 2008, Thousand Oaks, CA: Corwin Press. © 2008 Corwin Press. Used with permission.

Figure 3: Maria's Sample Student Survey

STUDENT SURVEY: WHO AM I AS A READER?

1. List five different types of things that you read.

1. The Harry Potter Novels

2. Short Stories

3. Shel Silverstein poetry

4. The Lion, the witch, and the wardrobe

5. Art books

V L S M B P I N

4. Draw a face that shows how you feel about reading and explain what your face means.

I'm happy! My face shows that my eyes are closed but I'm still seeing what's happening on the movie screen in my head. I hear the words too!

V L S M B P I N

2. What are some things you do to help you understand what you're reading when you read?

I close my eyes and try to imagine what is happening in my mind.

I listen closely to the way poetry sounds. Sometimes it's almost like hearing music and all of a sudden you just get it!

V L S M B P I N

3. Is reading for you more like climbing a mountain, riding a bike, going on a picnic, or watching a movie?

Choose one option and explain your choice below.

It's definitely like watching a movie. The best way to get it is to see it in your head. You can imagine all the characters and what they look like and what they're doing.

V L S M B P I N

MASTERY

INTERPERSONAL

UNDERSTANDING

SELF-EXPRESSIVE

Figure 4: Colin's Sample Student Survey

STUDENT SURVEY: WHO AM I AS A READER?

MASTERY

1. List five different types of things that you read.

1. Guiness Book of World Records
2. Articles about famous people
3. Trivia and fact books
4. Video game tips and hints
5. Books that show you how to make things

V L S M B P I N

INTERPERSONAL

4. Draw a face that shows how you feel about reading and explain what your face means.

Reading's OK. It helps you get what you need, but I'm not going crazy over it. So my face has a little smile.

V L S M B P I N

UNDERSTANDING

2. What are some things you do to help you understand what you're reading when you read?

• I quiz myself to make sure I remember what I just read

• I underline important facts

V L S M B P I N

SELF-EXPRESSIVE

3. Is reading for you more like climbing a mountain, riding a bike, going on a picnic, or watching a movie?

Choose one option and explain your choice below.

Reading is most like climbing a mountain. You do the work and you reach your goal by getting to the top faster than anyone else.

V L S M B P I N

Why Do Reading Styles Matter?

1. Styles are the key to motivating readers.

Take a second look at the four styles of readers described in Figure 2 (p. 9). Which style sounds most like you? Which style of reading gives you the most trouble? Now consider a few of your students. Which styles are strong? Which styles are underdeveloped? The reason behind these questions is simple: when we pay attention to our students' reading styles, patterns of strength and weakness come into sharp focus. This means that addressing students' reading styles enables you to motivate all of the young readers in your classroom. The trick is to help students tap into their natural strengths by providing instruction and activities that enlist their dominant styles. At the same time, by incorporating all four styles into your instruction and assessment, you also encourage your students to "stretch"—to try out new ways of thinking and grow their underdeveloped capacities.

2. Different texts make different demands on readers.

Thanks to our style preferences, some texts tend to challenge us more than others. To see why, take two very different texts, say a Shel Silverstein poem and a section from a mathematics textbook demonstrating how to make change using coins. Appreciating the language and imagery of Shel Silverstein calls for an entirely different kind of thinking than trying to internalize the steps in a mathematical procedure. Similarly, the thinking processes involved in understanding scientific phenomena will not be terribly useful when it comes to reading a story that asks readers to empathize with immigrants arriving at Ellis Island. The different thinking processes involved in appreciating poetry, memorizing procedures, identifying with content, and developing explanations require different styles of thinking and reading.

If each text highlighted a particular style of reading, that would be reason enough to develop students' capacities to think and read in all four styles. But the truth is, most texts operate on multiple levels. Students cannot simply read one text for its power to stir the imagination, another for its factual information, a third for its emotional impact, and a fourth for the coherence of its explanation. Often, a single text requires all of these types of reading.

For example, imagine a fairly typical elementary-school reading, say an article from a kid-friendly periodical discussing the problems that Florida manatees face. In all likelihood, the article would

- Detail the *What* or the facts of the situation (e.g., the estimated number of Florida manatees in existence, where they are concentrated, what's being done to help them, etc.).

- Explain the *Why* of the situation (e.g., the causes behind the decline in population).

- Imagine *What if?* (e.g., exploring what might happen ecologically if the Florida manatee is driven to extinction).

- Highlight the personal and emotional aspects of the content by eliciting sympathy for the Florida manatee.

Reading in all four styles, then, is essential to deep understanding. The best readers, whether consciously or unconsciously, know how to use all four styles (see Figure 5).

Figure 5: Reading in All Four Styles

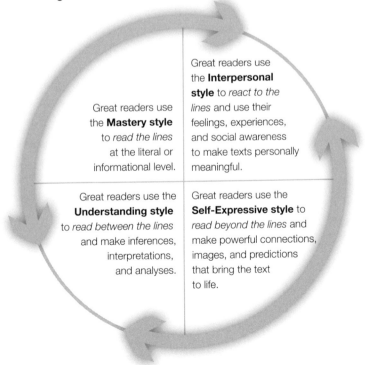

Great readers use the **Mastery style** to *read the lines* at the literal or informational level.

Great readers use the **Interpersonal style** to *react to the lines* and use their feelings, experiences, and social awareness to make texts personally meaningful.

Great readers use the **Understanding style** to *read between the lines* and make inferences, interpretations, and analyses.

Great readers use the **Self-Expressive style** to *read beyond the lines* and make powerful connections, images, and predictions that bring the text to life.

3. Self-aware readers are more proficient readers.

Styles are not just for teachers. Invite your students into the conversation about the different ways of reading and help them to identify their strong and underdeveloped styles. If you do, you'll be doing your students a huge favor. Research shows that when students are encouraged to reflect on their successes and struggles, exchange ideas for overcoming challenges with the teacher and other students, and target areas for improvement, their proficiency as readers and learners increases dramatically. Reading styles offer students and teachers a user-friendly framework for identifying strengths and weaknesses as well as a common language for discussing the complexities of the reading process.

4. Reading styles make the important work of differentiating reading instruction meaningful for students and manageable for teachers.

When we look at the four reading styles, we are, in effect, looking at a map for differentiating reading instruction. To ensure that you are reaching all styles of readers, you need to provide activities and ask questions that engage the different styles. Over the course of your lessons and units, rotate around the "wheel of style" so that all students are equally engaged by activities in their preferred styles and encouraged to try out new ways of thinking through activities in less-preferred styles. The "Question Menu" (Figure 6, p. 16) outlines the kinds of thinking associated with each style and provides a set of stems or question starters for developing your own questions in style.

One of the greatest benefits of this style-based approach to reading is how manageable the task of differentiating reading instruction becomes for the teacher. While many approaches to differentiation try to integrate all the ways students can be different and end up overwhelming the teacher, this approach focuses teachers' attention on the four styles of readers they will find in their classrooms.

5. Encouraging students to process information in different ways improves achievement.

The evidence for this statement can be found in a series of studies conducted by Dr. Robert Sternberg and his colleagues (as cited in Sternberg, 2006). In these studies, students were taught using five different instructional approaches:

- A memory-based approach emphasizing recall of facts and concepts

- An analytical approach emphasizing critical thinking and comparative analysis

- A creative approach emphasizing imagination and invention

- A practical approach emphasizing the application of concepts to real-world situations

- A diverse approach that incorporated all of these approaches

In these studies, students who were taught through an approach that matched their own style of learning almost always did better than students who were mismatched. But the more significant finding was this: students who were taught using a variety of approaches outperformed all other students. They did better on memory drills, they did better on objective tests, and they did better on performance assessments. Sternberg (2006) explains that multi-style teaching is effective because it "enables students to capitalize on their strengths and to correct or to compensate for their weaknesses, encoding material in a variety of interesting ways" (p. 34).

Figure 6: Question Menu

**Mastery questions
ask students to…**

Recall facts and find specific details:

- Who? What? Where?
  When? How?
- List three facts you learned about
  _____.

Describe and retell:

- Can you describe how it works?
- Can you retell or summarize
  what happened?

Sequence:

- What are the steps?
- In what order does the process
  happen?

**Interpersonal questions
ask students to…**

Empathize and describe feelings:

- How would you feel if _____
  happened to you? How do you
  think _____ felt?
- What decision would you make?
- Can you reflect on your own
  thoughts and feelings?
- Can you reflect on your own
  reading process?

Value and appreciate:

- Why is _____ important
  to you?
- What's the value of _____?
- Can you connect this to your
  own life?

Explore human-interest problems:

- How would you advise or console
  _____?
- How would you help each side
  come to an agreement?

**Understanding questions
ask students to…**

Find or construct main ideas:

- What are the two biggest ideas in
  the text?
- What is the main idea of the
  reading?
- Can you make a headline for the
  reading?

Analyze and explain:

- What are the key similarities and
  differences?
- Why? Can you explain it?
- What evidence supports your
  position?

Draw conclusions:

- What conclusions can you draw?
- What does the author mean by
  _____?

**Self-Expressive questions
ask students to…**

*Explain metaphorically or
symbolically:*

- How is _____ like
  _____?
- Develop a metaphor for
  _____.

*Develop images, hypotheses,
and predictions:*

- What would happen if
  _____?
- Can you imagine _____?
  What would it look/be like?
- Can you make a prediction?

Develop original products:

- Create a poem, icon, skit, or
  sculpture to represent _____.

Source: Adapted from *Reading for Academic Success, Grades 2-6: Differentiated Strategies for Struggling, Average, and Advanced Readers* (p. 221), by R. W. Strong, H. F. Silver, and M. J. Perini, 2008, Thousand Oaks, CA: Corwin Press. © 2008 Corwin Press. Used with permission.

But Didn't You Also Mention Multiple Intelligences?

While reading styles represent the central concept of this book, style is not the only model of cognitive diversity that informs the activities within it. The second model, multiple intelligences, has a more recent past than learning styles. But like learning styles, multiple intelligences have led to their own revolution in education and changes in how we think about differences among our students.

The theory of multiple intelligences was developed by Howard Gardner (1983/2011, 1999), who showed that traditional notions of intelligence, such as IQ testing, were inadequate when it came to explaining the great range of human achievement and problem-solving capacities. Why, Gardner wondered, were we insisting on a definition of intelligence that overlooked the work of parents, painters, preachers, pianists, pilots, philosophers, and so many other contributors to our culture? Drawing from the fields of neuroscience, cultural studies, literature, and history, Gardner has identified not one, but eight distinct forms of human intelligence. (See Figure 7 on page 18.)

Because each intelligence represents a "way to be smart," multiple intelligences give teachers another way to reach out to their students. Teachers can use multiple intelligences to engage more students in meaningful learning.

One way to address multiple intelligences is to make connections to other content areas and disciplines. Often, we can help our students get a better grasp on what they are learning by allowing them to explore content through the lens of a preferred intelligence. For example, middle-school science teacher Carl Carrozza (1996) explains how he uses multiple intelligences to help students learn rigorous science content: "With the help of Gardner's model, I have found it possible to link learning between different disciplines so that the student who loves music, for example, might be able to explore the scientific concepts of a piano or a series of sound waves that create melody, while the athlete might understand how an exercise regimen is scientifically grounded" (p. 146).

Figure 7: The Eight Intelligences

1. Verbal-Linguistic intelligence involves words and language. It is revealed in an ability to comprehend the spoken and written word and to communicate well through language.

2. Logical-Mathematical intelligence involves numbers and logic. It is revealed in an ability to reason, sequence, and identify both conceptual and numerical patterns.

3. Spatial intelligence involves pictures and images. It is revealed in an acute ability to perceive and transform visual and spatial information, a talent that involves sensitivity to detail and orientation.

4. Musical intelligence involves music and sound. It is revealed in a sensitive perception of the auditory world.

5. Bodily-Kinesthetic intelligence involves physicality and movement. It is revealed in conceptual control of one's body and the immediate world.

6. Interpersonal intelligence involves human relationships. It is revealed in an ability to understand others, to perceive and effectively respond to the moods of others.

7. Intrapersonal intelligence involves the inner self. It is revealed in the ability to access and discriminate personal feelings and emotional states.

8. Naturalist* intelligence involves making sense of the natural world. It is revealed in the ability to recognize, discriminate among, and classify living things and natural objects.

*__*Note:__ The naturalist intelligence was not part of Gardner's original seven intelligences. Gardner introduced the naturalist intelligence in* Intelligence Reframed *(1999). In his third edition of* Frames of Mind *(2011), Gardner remains committed to the naturalist intelligence but does not discuss it at length.*

Multiple intelligences are also ideal for allowing students to demonstrate what they know in a variety of ways. There are many ways for students to show what they know. If we expect to assess students' understanding, we need more than tests and essays; we need an assessment system driven by realistic problems and questions that engage students in authentic performances and the creation of meaningful products. Multiple intelligences, with their emphasis on the contributions that people with diverse talents make to our culture, suggest a wide range of meaningful products and performances that can serve as the basis for assessment.

Take a look at the menu below (Figure 8). Can you think of any other products or performances within the various intelligences that are not listed?

Figure 8: Menu of Products/Performances by Multiple Intelligences

Verbal-Linguistic Products: Debates, journals, conferences, presentations, essays, poems, plays, articles, interpretations, explanations, fables, letters, interviews, newscasts, text-based web pages and presentations, blogs

Logical-Mathematical Products: Budgets, predictions, analyses, computer programs, experiments, arguments, mathematical problems, applications, court cases

Spatial Products: Maps, charts, tables, brochures, ads, flowcharts, design analyses, artistic projects, cartoons, comic strips, diagrams, museum exhibits, posters, collages, websites, animations

Musical Products: Musical analyses, raps, jingles, blues, musical performances, investigating musical issues, digital music production

Bodily-Kinesthetic Products: Plays, dramatic sketches, dance, building/repairing, sculptures, hands-on demonstrations

Interpersonal Products: Investigating social or psychological issues, psychological analyses (e.g., of fictional characters), community projects, surveys, interviews, conferences, motivational speeches, teaching concepts to others, social networking

Intrapersonal Products: Artistic projects, diaries, journals, goal-setting activities, projects involving personal choice, independent study, reflection activities, memoirs, online journals

Naturalist Products: Ecological analyses or problem-solving, experiments, taxonomies, environmental studies, caring for plants or animals

So, How Do I Put Reading Styles and Multiple Intelligences to Work in My Classroom?

This book has been designed to help you put the power of reading styles and multiple intelligences to work in your classroom easily and without making fundamental changes to what you already do. What you'll find in this book is a collection of Task Rotations in three different genres—fiction, nonfiction, and poetry. Task Rotations (Silver & Hanson, 1998; Silver, Jackson, & Moirao, 2011) allow students to interact thoughtfully with a text by giving students the opportunity to respond to what they read in all four styles. These Task Rotations help students draw out the unique qualities of individual texts, whether the text is a humorous poem, a mystery story, or an article on a newly discovered deep-sea creature. In addition, each Task Rotation is aligned with the Common Core State Standards, helping teachers address key reading, writing, speaking and listening, and language standards in ways that students enjoy.

Let's take a closer look at a one of the Task Rotations you'll find in this book (Figure 9, p. 21). Each Task Rotation includes

1. A **Common Core Corner** noting alignment with the Common Core State Standards (see p. 39 for more information).

2. A brief introduction to the Task Rotation written in student-friendly language.

3. Clear and simple directions for students to complete each task.

4. Four interrelated tasks, one in each style.

5. "Can't-miss" reminders that identify the style of each task.

6. A multiple intelligences indicator showing which intelligences are engaged by each task.

The specific intelligences used in the task are indicated in a bold font according to the key below:

V = *Verbal-Linguistic Intelligence*   **B** = *Bodily-Kinesthetic Intelligence*

L = *Logical-Mathematical Intelligence*   **P** = *Interpersonal Intelligence*

S = *Spatial Intelligence*   **I** = *Intrapersonal Intelligence*

M = *Musical Intelligence*   **N** = *Naturalist Intelligence*

Figure 9: What's in a Task Rotation?

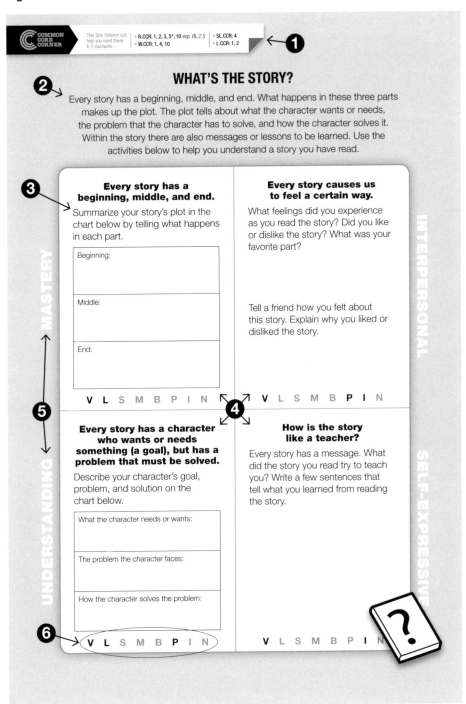

COMMON CORE CORNER

This Task Rotation can help you meet these K–5 standards.

> R.CCR: 1, 2, 3, 5*, 10 *esp. RL.2.5*
> W.CCR: 1, 4, 10
> SL.CCR: 4
> L.CCR: 1, 2

WHAT'S THE STORY?

Every story has a beginning, middle, and end. What happens in these three parts makes up the plot. The plot tells about what the character wants or needs, the problem that the character has to solve, and how the character solves it. Within the story there are also messages or lessons to be learned. Use the activities below to help you understand a story you have read.

MASTERY

Every story has a beginning, middle, and end.

Summarize your story's plot in the chart below by telling what happens in each part.

Beginning:

Middle:

End:

V **L** S M B P I N

INTERPERSONAL

Every story causes us to feel a certain way.

What feelings did you experience as you read the story? Did you like or dislike the story? What was your favorite part?

Tell a friend how you felt about this story. Explain why you liked or disliked the story.

V L S M B **P** I N

UNDERSTANDING

Every story has a character who wants or needs something (a goal), but has a problem that must be solved.

Describe your character's goal, problem, and solution on the chart below.

What the character needs or wants:

The problem the character faces:

How the character solves the problem:

V **L** S M B **P** I N

SELF-EXPRESSIVE

How is the story like a teacher?

Every story has a message. What did the story you read try to teach you? Write a few sentences that tell what you learned from reading the story.

V L S M B P I N

In the remainder of this book, you will find

- **Classroom Connections:** Remember those activities you completed in this introduction? Student-friendly versions of all of these activities appear in the next section. These activities are great ways to introduce students to the concept of reading styles before you begin using Task Rotations in the classroom.

- **Using Task Rotations to Address Common Core State Standards**, which includes a Common Core Alignment Index for locating Task Rotations that address specific Common Core State Standards.

- **Fiction Task Rotations** that will help students develop their understanding of elements like plot, characters, and setting.

- **Nonfiction Task Rotations** that will help students learn how to read informational texts, find main ideas, and conduct research.

- **Poetry Task Rotations** that will help students appreciate different kinds of poetry and learn how poets express ideas and feelings.

- **Designing Task Rotations for Your Classroom**, which is dedicated to showing you how to create your own Task Rotations to meet specific standards and objectives.

With thoughtful reading strategies such as Task Rotation in the hands of dedicated professionals like you, we can all be sure that our students will become active, confident, and independent readers.

Enjoy and happy reading!

Classroom Connections

REPRODUCIBLE ACTIVITIES
FOR USE IN YOUR CLASSROOM

In this section, you'll find a collection of classroom-ready activities to engage students in the process of discovering their own reading preferences and styles. These activities correspond to those marked by a Classroom Connection icon in the introduction. Use these pages and activities with your students to introduce key concepts like reading styles and Task Rotation and to support the development of their reading and thinking skills. These Classroom Connections—and other select reproducible pages—are available for download from our online Reading Style Resource Center at www.ThoughtfulClassroom.com/ReadingResources.

> ***Student Survey Note:** Consider asking your students to complete this student survey twice—both before they begin working with tasks in style and after they've had some experience using all four styles to respond to readings. Using this survey as a pre- and post-learning activity is a great way to help students notice and reflect on their evolution as readers and thinkers.

WHAT ARE YOU LIKE AS A READER?

1

Have you ever thought about who you are as a reader? You might already think of yourself as a friend, an athlete, an artist. Anyone who reads is also a reader, including you!

We all read, but we read in different ways. We have our own thoughts while we read. We often remember different parts of a book or website than others who read the same thing.

We call the different ways people read *reading styles*. You will be doing several activities that help you think about yourself as a reader and discover your reading style. Learning about your reading style and using your new knowledge will help you meet any reading challenge, now and throughout your life!

Let's try the first of these activities right now, an activity called "What Are You Like as a Reader?"

A ritual is a set of actions that you like to do the same way over time. Rituals are patterns in your daily life that help you feel comfortable. Most people follow certain rituals before they leave the house in the morning, go to bed at night, or pack for a trip. Most people also have reading rituals.

So, what reading rituals do you have? Can you read anywhere, or do you have a special place or a special chair or a special desk just for reading? Does the time of day matter to you? Do you find that you read better in the morning, the afternoon, or the evening? Are you able to read when there is a lot of background noise or do you prefer total silence? Would you rather read alone or in a crowded library or classroom where other people are reading?

Use the space on your worksheet to list any reading rituals you have.

WHAT ARE YOU LIKE AS A READER?

Use the space below to list any reading rituals you have.

My Reading Rituals...

2

THE IMAGINARY BOOKSTORE

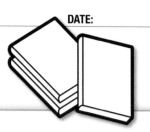

1

Here's another way to think about who you are as a reader. Imagine that you enter a brand new bookstore in your town. You see a sign that says, "Readers, This Way!" You turn a corner and walk into a room with thousands of books and colorful book covers everywhere you look—it's a feast for the eyes. You have some money in your pocket and time to spend as well. But how do you find the book you want? Where's the directory? That's when you look up and see the largest and most unusual bookstore directory you've ever seen.

Welcome to the Wonderful World of Reading

Books Containing Useful Information

- How-To Books
- Encyclopedias, Almanacs, World Records, and Other Reference Texts
- Information Guides and Manuals

"Get the knowledge you need—instantly!"

Books About People

- Biographies and Autobiographies
- Stories About Friendship and Teamwork
- Overcoming Personal Challenges

"Celebrate the human spirit!"

Books That Make You Think

- Science and Technology
- Books That Explain Unusual Events and Why Things Happen
- Mysteries and Puzzles
- Classic Stories

"Get the wheels in your mind turning!"

Books That Stir the Imagination

- Fantasy and Science Fiction
- Poetry
- Art
- Mystery, Fables, and Folktales

"Spark your creativity!"

THE IMAGINARY BOOKSTORE

Think about the unusual bookstore directory and answer the questions below.

2

So, which way do you go?

Which path would you avoid?

What might your choices say about you as a reader?

HOW DO YOU READ?

1

It's probably not too difficult for you to talk about the kinds of books you like to read. But do you know *how* you read?

Different people have different ways of reading. Some readers like to hunt down specific pieces of information. Some readers are great at making pictures or movies in their minds as they read. Some readers love to think through challenging ideas. Some readers like to make connections to their own experiences as they read.

In the box on the next page, you'll find twelve different reading behaviors, or ways of reading. All readers use all these behaviors. But it's also true that most of us prefer certain behaviors over others. Carefully read the twelve behaviors in the box. Which behaviors seem to describe you best as a reader? Which sound least like what you do as you read? Pick the three behaviors that you think best describe you as a reader. Put a symbol like a smiley face (☺), star (☆), or check mark (✓) next to the three behaviors that best describe you as a reader.

HOW DO YOU READ?

Read each statement in the boxes below. Put a symbol like a smiley face (☺), star (☆), or a check mark (✓) next to the three behaviors that best describe you as a reader.

2

Mastery

____ I track down specific information.

____ I focus on the important details.

____ I stop and make sure I remember what I've read.

Interpersonal

____ I try to think what I would do if I were the character.

____ I try to make connections between what I'm reading and my own experiences.

____ I want to hear what other people think about the reading.

Understanding

____ I make sure I understand the big ideas.

____ I think of questions I'd like to ask the author.

____ I ask myself what the author is trying to tell me.

Self-Expressive

____ I look for new and interesting ways the author uses words.

____ I make pictures and movies in my mind to help me imagine what's happening.

____ I try to predict what will happen next.

Take a look at the four boxes. Can you find a pattern? Does one box have two or three symbols in it? If so, this may give you some clues about your reading style.

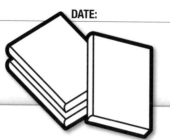

WHAT ARE READING STYLES?

1

We call the different ways people read *reading styles*. All readers use all four styles to help them read, but most readers tend to be especially strong in one or two of these styles. Look at the chart below. Which of the four boxes sounds most like you? Put a star (☆) in the box that sounds most like you.

You're probably a strong Mastery reader if you...

- Read because you want to learn information you can use.
- Like readings that are clear and useful.
- Like questions that ask you to recall information from the reading.

You're probably a strong Interpersonal reader if you...

- Read because you want to understand yourself and other people.
- Like readings that focus on feelings, friendship, and overcoming challenges.
- Like questions that ask you how you feel or what you would do if you were a character in the reading.

You're probably a strong Understanding reader if you...

- Read because you want to be challenged to think.
- Like readings that focus on new ways of thinking.
- Like questions that ask you to explain, prove, or take a position on the ideas in the reading.

You're probably a strong Self-Expressive reader if you...

- Read because you want to use your imagination.
- Like readings that are creative.
- Like questions that ask you to imagine and predict.

? Does the box you've picked in this chart match the box with the most symbols in it from the "How Do You Read?" activity?

WHAT ARE READING STYLES?

Read each question below and write down your thoughts in the blank spaces.

Find a partner who selected a different box than you did. Talk about how your reading styles differ. How could talking with someone who has a different reading style help you as a reader? Write down your thoughts here.

2

Which reading style would you like to become better at using? How do you think that would help you as a reader?

Thinking about your reading style is a great way to get a better sense of who you are as a reader and what your strengths are.

Remember...

- Most of what you will read in life requires you to use all four styles.

- Knowing about your reading style will help you use your strengths and focus on ways to improve as a reader.

- You can learn more about reading when you talk with friends and teachers.

- You can use your knowledge to become a great reader for life!

WHAT'S A TASK ROTATION?

1

One of the goals of understanding reading styles is to learn how to become a more powerful reader who can think and read well in all four styles.

A Task Rotation includes four tasks or activities that ask you to read, write, and think about a particular reading using all four reading styles. By responding to what you've read in different ways, you'll become a stronger and more well-rounded reader. Think of your teacher as a coach, and yourself as a reading athlete-in-training. The Task Rotations are exercises that help you gain strength and flexibility as a reader.

Task Rotations ask you to respond to readings in the following ways:

Mastery tasks ask you to remember, describe, and find specific information.	**Interpersonal tasks** ask you to explore your feelings and personal reactions to the text.
Understanding tasks ask you to give reasons and explain.	**Self-Expressive tasks** ask you to imagine and create.

WHAT'S A TASK ROTATION?

For example, let's imagine you've just finished reading an article on dinosaurs and your teacher wants you to show what you know by completing this Task Rotation.

2

Mastery Task	Interpersonal Task
Make a list of three important things you learned from the text about dinosaurs.	Tell a friend what you learned from reading that he or she might not know.
Understanding Task	**Self-Expressive Task**
Why do you think the author wrote this piece about dinosaurs? What big idea was she trying to tell us?	Create a picture that will help you remember what you have learned from reading about dinosaurs.

Your teacher will give you directions on how to complete different Task Rotations at different times. You may be asked to complete the tasks in a specific order, or you may be given a choice about the order for completing the activities.

STUDENT SURVEY

1

Reading is not an activity limited to books. Wherever there are words, there is reading to be done!

Read through and complete the activities on the next page to get a better picture of who you are as a reader. You'll also find two different samples of other students' work to help you see how other readers have completed this survey.

Your teacher may ask you to complete these four activities again during the school year, depending on what you are reading and learning. Completing this survey later in the year may help you see how you've grown as a reader.

STUDENT SURVEY: WHO AM I AS A READER?

MASTERY

UNDERSTANDING

1. List five different types of things that you read.

   1.

   2.

   3.

   4.

   5.

V L S M B P I N

4. Draw a face that shows how you feel about reading and explain what your face means.

V L S M B P I N

2. What are some things you do to help you understand what you're reading when you read?

V L S M B P I N

3. Is reading for you more like climbing a mountain, riding a bike, going on a picnic, or watching a movie?

Choose one option and explain your choice below.

V L S M B P I N

2

INTERPERSONAL

SELF-EXPRESSIVE

SAMPLE STUDENT SURVEY

STUDENT SURVEY: WHO AM I AS A READER?

MASTERY

1. List five different types of things that you read.

1. The Harry Potter Novels
2. Short Stories
3. Shel Silverstein poetry
4. The Lion, the witch, and the wardrobe
5. Art books

V L S M B P I N

INTERPERSONAL

4. Draw a face that shows how you feel about reading and explain what your face means.

I'm happy!

My face shows that my eyes are closed but I'm still seeing what's happening on the movie screen in my head. I hear the words too!

V L S M B P I N

UNDERSTANDING

2. What are some things you do to help you understand what you're reading when you read?

I close my eyes and try to imagine what is happening in my mind.

I listen closely to the way poetry sounds. Sometimes it's almost like hearing music and all of a sudden you just get it!

V L S M B P I N

SELF-EXPRESSIVE

3. Is reading for you more like climbing a mountain, riding a bike, going on a picnic, or watching a movie?

Choose one option and explain your choice below.

It's definitely like watching a movie. The best way to get it is to see it in your head. You can imagine all the characters and what they look like and what they're doing.

V L S M B P I N

SAMPLE STUDENT SURVEY

STUDENT SURVEY: WHO AM I AS A READER?

4

MASTERY

1. List five different types of things that you read.

1. Guiness Book of World Records
2. Articles about famous people
3. Trivia and fact books
4. Video game tips and hints
5. Books that show you how to make things

V L S M B P I N

INTERPERSONAL

4. Draw a face that shows how you feel about reading and explain what your face means.

Reading's OK. It helps you get what you need, but I'm not going crazy over it. So my face has a little smile.

V L S M B P I N

UNDERSTANDING

2. What are some things you do to help you understand what you're reading when you read?

• I quiz myself to make sure I remember what I just read

• I underline important facts

V L S M B P I N

SELF-EXPRESSIVE

3. Is reading for you more like climbing a mountain, riding a bike, going on a picnic, or watching a movie?

Choose one option and explain your choice below.

Reading is most like climbing a mountain. You do the work and you reach your goal by getting to the top faster than anyone else.

V L S M B P I N

Using
Task Rotations
to Address
Common Core State Standards

This section highlights two features of this book designed to help teachers address Common Core State Standards: the **Common Core Corner** and the **Common Core Alignment Index**.

Common Core Corner

Each Task Rotation in this book comes with a standards correlation tool called a Common Core Corner (as seen below).

COMMON CORE CORNER — This Task Rotation can help you meet these K-5 standards…
> R.CCR: 1, 2, 3, 5*, 10 *esp. RL.2.5*
> W.CCR: 1, 4, 10
> SL.CCR: 4
> L.CCR: 1, 2

The purpose of the Common Core Corner is to tell you which College and Career Readiness Anchor Standards (known simply as "Anchor Standards") in Reading (R.CCR), Writing (W.CCR), Speaking and Listening (SL.CCR), and Language (L.CCR) a particular Task Rotation can help you address.

For example, the Common Core Corner above goes with the Task Rotation called "What's the Story?" (p. 46). This Common Core Corner indicates that this Task Rotation can help you address Anchor Standards 1, 2, 3, 5, and 10 in Reading, Anchor Standards 1, 4, and 10 in Writing, Anchor Standard 4 in Speaking and Listening, and Anchor Standards 1 and 2 in Language. Task Rotations are aligned with Anchor Standards (rather than grade-specific standards) because Task Rotations are designed to be used at multiple grade levels and adapted freely by teachers; however, some Task Rotations align particularly well with grade-specific standards. In these cases, the Anchor Standard is followed by an asterisk (*) and the relevant grade-specific standard is identified to the right. For example, "*esp. RL.2.5*" in the Common Core Corner above tells you that this Task Rotation addresses standard 5 in the Reading Literature strand at grade 2 particularly well. To learn more about the Common Core State Standards and how they're organized and coded, visit www.corestandards.org.

Common Core Alignment Index

In addition to the Common Core Corner that comes with each Task Rotation, you can also refer to the Common Core Alignment Index below (pp. 40-42). Use this index to help you key in on particular Anchor Standards and then locate the Task Rotations that can help you address these standards. Because the Common Core Alignment Index includes the full text of each Anchor Standard (from www.corestandards.org), you can use it as a quick reference guide any time you need to recall a specific Anchor Standard.

Code	College and Career Readiness Anchor Standards for Reading	Task Rotation Pages
	Key Ideas and Details	
R.CCR.1	1. Read closely to determine what the text says explicitly and to make logical inferences from it; cite specific textual evidence when writing or speaking to support conclusions drawn from the text.	45, 46, 47, 48, 49, 50, 55, 56, 57, 58, 59, 60, 61, 68
R.CCR.2	2. Determine central ideas or themes of a text and analyze their development; summarize the key supporting details and ideas.	45, 46, 49, 50, 51, 56, 57, 61
R.CCR.3	3. Analyze how and why individuals, events, and ideas develop and interact over the course of a text.	45, 46, 47, 48, 49, 59
	Craft and Structure	
R.CCR.4	4. Interpret words and phrases as they are used in a text, including determining technical, connotative, and figurative meanings, and analyze how specific word choices shape meaning or tone.	65, 66, 67, 68
R.CCR.5	5. Analyze the structure of texts, including how specific sentences, paragraphs, and larger portions of the text (e.g., a section, chapter, scene, or stanza) relate to each other and the whole.	46, 51, 55, 65, 69
R.CCR.6	6. Assess how point of view or purpose shapes the content and style of a text.	48, 49, 50, 56, 58
	Integration of Knowledge and Ideas	
R.CCR.7	7. Integrate and evaluate content presented in diverse media and formats, including visually and quantitatively, as well as in words.	49, 55, 56, 61
R.CCR.8	8. Delineate and evaluate the argument and specific claims in a text, including the validity of the reasoning as well as the relevance and sufficiency of the evidence.	58, 59, 60
R.CCR.9	9. Analyze how two or more texts address similar themes or topics in order to build knowledge or to compare the approaches the authors take.	55, 61, 69
	Range of Reading and Level of Text Complexity	
R.CCR.10	10. Read and comprehend complex literary and informational texts independently and proficiently.	45, 46, 47, 48, 49, 50, 51, 55, 56, 57, 58, 59, 60, 61, 65, 66, 67, 68, 69

For the complete Common Core State Standards go to www.corestandards.org.

Code	College and Career Readiness Anchor Standards for Writing	Task Rotation Pages
Text Types and Purposes		
W.CCR.1	1. Write arguments to support claims in an analysis of substantive topics or texts, using valid reasoning and relevant and sufficient evidence.	46, 50, 55, 59, 60, 66, 67, 68, 69
W.CCR.2	2. Write informative/explanatory texts to examine and convey complex ideas and information clearly and accurately through the effective selection, organization, and analysis of content.	47, 49, 56, 67
W.CCR.3	3. Write narratives to develop real or imagined experiences or events using effective technique, well-chosen details, and well-structured event sequences.	51, 58, 61
Production and Distribution of Writing		
W.CCR.4	4. Produce clear and coherent writing in which the development, organization, and style are appropriate to task, purpose, and audience.	46, 51, 58, 59, 60, 66, 67
W.CCR.5	5. Develop and strengthen writing as needed by planning, revising, editing, rewriting, or trying a new approach.	58
W.CCR.6	6. Use technology, including the Internet, to produce and publish writing and to interact and collaborate with others.	*see note below*
Research to Build and Present Knowledge		
W.CCR.7	7. Conduct short as well as more sustained research projects based on focused questions, demonstrating understanding of the subject under investigation.	61
W.CCR.8	8. Gather relevant information from multiple print and digital sources, assess the credibility and accuracy of each source, and integrate the information while avoiding plagiarism.	61
W.CCR.9	9. Draw evidence from literary or informational texts to support analysis, reflection, and research.	48, 49, 60, 61
Range of Writing		
W.CCR.10	10. Write routinely over extended time frames (time for research, reflection, and revision) and shorter time frames (a single sitting or a day or two) for a range of tasks, purposes, and audiences.	46, 47, 48, 49, 50, 51, 55, 56, 59, 60, 65, 66, 67, 68, 69

*Note: Although this standard is not addressed directly, most Task Rotation activities in this book can be enhanced through online publishing and collaboration tools.

Code	College and Career Readiness Anchor Standards for Speaking and Listening	Task Rotation Pages
	Comprehension and Collaboration	
SL.CCR.1	1. Prepare for and participate effectively in a range of conversations and collaborations with diverse partners, building on others' ideas and expressing their own clearly and persuasively.	51, 58
SL.CCR.2	2. Integrate and evaluate information presented in diverse media and formats, including visually, quantitatively, and orally.	51, 57
SL.CCR.3	3. Evaluate a speaker's point of view, reasoning, and use of evidence and rhetoric.	51, 58
	Presentation of Knowledge and Ideas	
SL.CCR.4	4. Present information, findings, and supporting evidence such that listeners can follow the line of reasoning and the organization, development, and style are appropriate to task, purpose, and audience.	46, 51, 56, 57
SL.CCR.5	5. Make strategic use of digital media and visual displays of data to express information and enhance understanding of presentations.	45, 47, 49, 56, 59, 65, 68
SL.CCR.6	6. Adapt speech to a variety of contexts and communicative tasks, demonstrating command of formal English when indicated or appropriate.	51, 56, 57

Code	College and Career Readiness Anchor Standards for Language	Task Rotation Pages
	Conventions of Standard English	
L.CCR.1	1. Demonstrate command of the conventions of standard English grammar and usage when writing or speaking.	46, 47, 48, 49, 50, 51, 55, 56, 57, 58, 59, 60, 61, 65, 66, 67, 68, 69
L.CCR.2	2. Demonstrate command of the conventions of standard English capitalization, punctuation, and spelling when writing.	46, 47, 48, 49, 50, 51, 55, 56, 58, 59, 60, 61, 65, 66, 67, 68, 69
	Knowledge of Language	
L.CCR.3	3. Apply knowledge of language to understand how language functions in different contexts, to make effective choices for meaning or style, and to comprehend more fully when reading or listening.	51, 66, 67
	Vocabulary Acquisition and Use	
L.CCR.4	4. Determine or clarify the meaning of unknown and multiple-meaning words and phrases by using context clues, analyzing meaningful word parts, and consulting general and specialized reference materials, as appropriate.	57
L.CCR.5	5. Demonstrate understanding of word relationships and nuances in word meanings.	55, 60, 65, 66, 67, 68
	Range of Writing	
L.CCR.6	6. Acquire and use accurately a range of general academic and domain-specific words and phrases sufficient for reading, writing, speaking, and listening at the college and career readiness level; demonstrate independence in gathering vocabulary knowledge when encountering an unknown term important to comprehension or expression.	48, 51, 58, 61

For the complete Common Core State Standards go to www.corestandards.org.

Fiction Task Rotations

While we encourage you to use the following Task Rotations in your classroom, they are meant to be something more than reproducibles. We like to think of them as models, ideas, inspiration—as "mind starters" you can use and modify to meet the needs of your students while sparking their passion to read.

Note: Full-size copies of select Task Rotations from this genre are available for download from the Reading Style Resource Center at www.ThoughtfulClassroom.com/ReadingResources.

This Task Rotation can help you meet these K-5 standards…

> R.CCR: 1, 2, 3, 10
> W.CCR: NA
> SL.CCR: 5
> L.CCR: NA

COMMON CORE CORNER

READERS, TAKE ACTION!

Good readers are active readers. As they read, good readers think about what is important, ask themselves questions, and try to find answers. They make predictions and visualize in their mind what is happening in the story. Select a book or story and try using some of the techniques from the **Mark**, **Ask**, **Predict**, and **See** process as you read.

MASTERY

Mark the Page

As you read, *underline*, *circle*, or *highlight* the ideas, details, and vocabulary words you think are important.

(Use sticky notes if you are not able to write directly on the text you are reading.)

V L S M B P I N

INTERPERSONAL

See It in Your Mind

When you read, try to see in your mind what is going on in the story. Stop reading to think about what you read. Then draw a picture of what you saw in your mind.

V L S M B P I N

UNDERSTANDING

Ask Questions

When you read, stop and ask yourself questions about what you are reading. List four questions you asked yourself as you read. Then record the answers you found.

	Question	Answer
1.		
2.		
3.		
4.		

V L S M B P I N

SELF-EXPRESSIVE

Make Predictions

When you read, try to predict what will happen next in the story. Stop reading, record your prediction, then continue reading to see if you were correct.

Prediction(s)	What Happened?

V L S M B P I N

COMMON CORE CORNER

This Task Rotation can help you meet these K-5 standards…

> R.CCR: 1, 2, 3, 5*, 10 *esp. RL.2.5*
> W.CCR: 1, 4, 10
> SL.CCR: 4
> L.CCR: 1, 2

WHAT'S THE STORY?

Every story has a beginning, middle, and end. What happens in these three parts makes up the plot. The plot tells about what the character wants or needs, the problem that the character has to solve, and how the character solves it. Within the story there are also messages or lessons to be learned. Use the activities below to help you understand a story you have read.

MASTERY

Every story has a beginning, middle, and end.

Summarize your story's plot in the chart below by telling what happens in each part.

| Beginning: |
| Middle: |
| End: |

V **L** S M B P I N

INTERPERSONAL

Every story causes us to feel a certain way.

What feelings did you experience as you read the story? Did you like or dislike the story? What was your favorite part?

Tell a friend how you felt about this story. Explain why you liked or disliked the story.

V L S M B **P** I N

UNDERSTANDING

Every story has a character who wants or needs something (a goal), but has a problem that must be solved.

Describe your character's goal, problem, and solution on the chart below.

| What the character needs or wants: |
| The problem the character faces: |
| How the character solves the problem: |

V **L** S M B **P** I N

SELF-EXPRESSIVE

How is the story like a teacher?

Every story has a message. What did the story you read try to teach you? Write a few sentences that tell what you learned from reading the story.

V **L** S M B P I N

?

This Task Rotation can help you meet these K-5 standards…
> R.CCR: 1, 3, 10
> W.CCR: 2, 10
> SL.CCR: 5
> L.CCR: 1, 2

COMMON CORE CORNER

WHERE AND WHEN?

Where does the story take place? When does it take place? If you can answer these questions, then you know the story's setting. As you read, look for clues that tell you where and when the story takes place. Then think about how the setting affects the story.

MASTERY

Setting the Scene

Collect some words that help you visualize the setting of the story.

What words tell about where the story takes place?

What words tell about when the story takes place?

V **L** S M B P I **N**

INTERPERSONAL

You and Your Setting

Different settings affect your behavior. Pick two types of settings and describe how you would act or behave in each.

in school   at home   with friends   with family
at the park   at the beach   at the movies

1.	2.

How would you act and behave in the setting in the story?

V **L** S M B P I **N**

UNDERSTANDING

What Does It Mean?

What role does the setting play in the story? Why is this setting an important part of the story?

V **L** S M B P I **N**

SELF-EXPRESSIVE

Imagine This

Change the setting of the story. Then draw a picture of the new setting. Explain how the new setting would affect the story.

V **L** S M B P I **N**

COMMON CORE CORNER

This Task Rotation can help you meet these K-5 standards…

> R.CCR: 1, 3, 6*, 10 *esp. RL.3.6*
> W.CCR: 9, 10
> SL.CCR: NA
> L.CCR: 1, 2, 6

WHAT A CHARACTER!

Characters are the people, animals, or other creatures in a story. You can learn about characters by what they say and do. Look for clues in what you read that help you figure out what the main character is like.

MASTERY

Say and Do

Make some notes on what the main character in the story says and does.

Character's Name: _____

Says	Does

V L S M B P I N

INTERPERSONAL

Describing You

Think about yourself. If you were a character in a story, what three adjectives would a reader use to describe you?

1.

2.

3.

Are you and the main character more alike or more different? Explain.

V L S M B P I N

Draw a picture of your character doing or saying something from the story.

V L S M B P I N

UNDERSTANDING

What Did You Learn?

Explain what you learned about the character from what he or she said and did in the story.

What are three adjectives you would use to describe the character?

1.

2.

3.

V L S M B P I N

SELF-EXPRESSIVE

Cinquain

Create a cinquain (five-line poem) to describe your character. The first line is the character's name. The second line contains two adjectives that describe the character. The third line has three action verbs ending in "-ing," which describe the character's actions. The fourth line is a four-word sentence or phrase about the character. Finally, the fifth line is a noun related to the character. *For example:*

Big Bad Wolf

angry   mean

huffing   puffing   blowing

Tries   to   catch   pigs

villain

V L S M B P I N

This Task Rotation can help you meet these K-5 standards...
> R.CCR: 1, 2, 3, 6, 7, 10
> W.CCR: 2, 9, 10
> SL.CCR: 5
> L.CCR: 1, 2

COMMON CORE CORNER

PROBLEM, SOLUTION

Stories often present a problem and tell how it gets solved. As you read a story, see if you can identify what the main character wants (goal), what his or her problem is, and how the problem is solved.

Problem?

Solution!

MASTERY

Character and Conflict

Who is the main character?

What does the main character want?

What problem does the main character need to solve?

V L S M B P I N

INTERPERSONAL

Learning from the Story

What did you learn from this story? How can it help you to solve a problem you might have?

V L S M B P I N

UNDERSTANDING

Problem Solver

Explain how the main character solves the problem in the story.

V L S M B P I N

SELF-EXPRESSIVE

Cover Story

Create a book cover for the story you read. On the cover, show the main character's problem or how it is solved. Explain why this is a good cover for the book.

V L S M B P I N

COMMON
CORE
CORNER

This Task Rotation can help you meet these K-5 standards…

> R.CCR: 1, 2, 6, 10
> W.CCR: 1, 10

> SL.CCR: NA
> L.CCR: 1, 2

WHAT'S YOUR OPINION?

When we read a story, we often have reactions to what we are reading. Select a story and record your reactions to what you read.

MASTERY

This Reminds Me of…

Does the story remind you of something else? List any books, movies, or personal experiences that remind you of this story.

V L S M B P I N

INTERPERSONAL

Feelings
What do you think of the story?

Rate the story by circling the reaction that best describes how you feel about the story.

• I really enjoyed the story.

• The story was OK.

• I didn't like the story.

Explain your choice.

V L S M B P I N

UNDERSTANDING

Message

In your opinion, what is the author's message?

Why do you think the author wrote this piece?

V L S M B P I N

SELF-EXPRESSIVE

Can You Make It Better?

Imagine you were the editor of this story. If you could change one thing in the story, what would it be? How would you change it?

V L S M B P I N

This Task Rotation can help you meet these K-5 standards…

> R.CCR: 2, 5, 10
> W.CCR: 3, 4, 10
> SL.CCR: 1, 2, 3, 4, 6
> L.CCR: 1, 2, 3, 6

COMMON CORE CORNER

CREATE YOUR OWN STORY

Stories are everywhere. We tell them to each other, we read them in books, we watch them play out on TV and in the movies. Stories entertain, teach, and help us learn about ourselves and other people. Use the activities below to help you develop your own story.

Parts of a Story

Think about a story you would like to write. Describe the beginning, middle, and end.

Beginning:

Middle:

End:

V L S M B P I N

Ask the Author

After you've written your story, meet with a small group and read your stories aloud. Lead a group discussion about your story. Make sure you discuss your story's parts, the message, and some words that helped your story come to life. *(Remember, you know your story best. If group members have some difficulty, try to give them hints.)*

V L S M B **P** I N

Your Story's Message

Stories have messages. What do you want people to learn from your story?

V L S M B **P** I N

Bring Your Story to Life

To make their stories more interesting, exciting, scary, or enjoyable, writers use different types of adjectives, verbs, and adverbs. Create a "Writer's Word Bank" that includes words you might use to help your story come to life.

V L S M B P I N

MASTERY

INTERPERSONAL

UNDERSTANDING

SELF-EXPRESSIVE

Nonfiction Task Rotations

While we encourage you to use the following Task Rotations in your classroom, they are meant to be something more than reproducibles. We like to think of them as models, ideas, inspiration—as "mind starters" you can use and modify to meet the needs of your students while sparking their passion to read.

Note: Full-size copies of select Task Rotations from this genre are available for download from the Reading Style Resource Center at www.ThoughtfulClassroom.com/ReadingResources.

This Task Rotation can help you meet these K-5 standards…

> R.CCR: 1, 5*, 7, 9, 10 *esp. RL.1.5*
> W.CCR: 1, 10
> SL.CCR: NA
> L.CCR: 1, 2, 5

COMMON CORE CORNER

WHAT IS NONFICTION?

The purpose of nonfiction is to provide information based on facts. Nonfiction writing is found everywhere… in newspapers, magazines, books, even in the directions for a game. Try the activities below to learn more about nonfiction.

MASTERY

Name It

Select four books from your library about animals: two nonfiction and two fiction. For each book, list the title and the author's name.

		Title	Author
Nonfiction	1.		
	2.		
Fiction	3.		
	4.		

V **L** **S** M B P I N

INTERPERSONAL

Which Do You Prefer?

Which do you think you like reading more: writing that gives you information about a topic (nonfiction) or stories that are made up (fiction)? Explain your preference.

V **L** S M B P **I** N

UNDERSTANDING

What's the Difference?

Examine these books carefully. Pay attention to the covers, titles, details, photos, illustrations, and sections. How are the two nonfiction texts similar? How do they differ from the fiction texts? Make a list of some of the features that might help you tell a nonfiction text from a work of fiction.

V **L** **S** M B P I N

SELF-EXPRESSIVE

Make a Connection
Nonfiction is to fiction as a horse is to a unicorn.

Create your own analogy to show your understanding of the relationship between nonfiction and fiction.

V **L** S M B P **I** N

This Task Rotation can help you meet these K-5 standards…

> R.CCR: 1, 2, 6*, 7, 10 *esp. RI.2.6*   > SL.CCR: 4, 5, 6
> W.CCR: 2, 10   > L.CCR: 1, 2

READING NONFICTION

Nonfiction writing teaches us new information. As you read, notice the important details and ideas. Ask yourself, What is the author trying to teach me? Make sure you complete the activities in order.

MASTERY

INTERPERSONAL

What I Learned

1. Make a list of important things you learned from the text.

V L S M B P I N

Did You Know?

4. Explain to a friend what you learned from reading this piece that you think he or she might not know. See if you can use your picture or sketch in your explanation.

V L S M B P I N

UNDERSTANDING

SELF-EXPRESSIVE

What's the Big Idea?

2. Explain why the author wrote the piece.

What big idea is the author trying to teach us?

V L S M B P I N

A Picture Helps You Remember

3. Create a picture or sketch that will help you remember what you learned from this piece.

V L S M B P I N

This Task Rotation can help you meet these K-5 standards…

> R.CCR: 1, 2, 10
> W.CCR: NA
> SL.CCR: 2, 4, 6
> L.CCR: 1, 4

COMMON CORE CORNER

WHAT'S THE BIG IDEA?

To understand what the author is saying, you need to look for the author's big idea and important details. Find an article to read and use the activities listed below to uncover the author's message. Make sure you complete the activities in order.

MASTERY

1. What is the author's topic? (What is the reading about?)

Identify and define three critical vocabulary words that help the reader understand the topic.

1.

2.

3.

V L S M B P I N

2. What do you believe is the single most important idea described in the reading?

List three facts or details that support this idea.

1.

2.

3.

V L S M B P I N

UNDERSTANDING

INTERPERSONAL

4. Look over your notes in boxes 1, 2, and 3. Meet with a friend. Put your notes away and retell the big idea and important details from the reading to your friend. Try to use all three vocabulary terms you identified in box 1 in your retelling.

V L S M B **P** I N

3. Create a web that connects your details to the big idea.

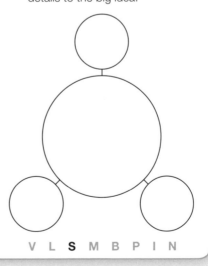

V L **S** M B P I N

SELF-EXPRESSIVE

This Task Rotation can help you meet these K-5 standards...

> R.CCR: 1, 6, 8*, 10 *esp. RI.3.8*
> W.CCR: 3, 4, 5
> SL.CCR: 1, 3
> L.CCR: 1, 2, 6

NONFICTION: SEQUENCE

Nonfiction writing that describes a sequence often uses transitional words like *first*, *second*, *next*, *then*, and *finally*. These words help readers follow the order of steps. Read a text that follows an order or describes a set of steps.

What sequence is described in the text? _____

MASTERY

Sequence and Steps

List the steps in order. Then turn your list of steps into a simple paragraph using transitional words like *first*, *second*, *next*, *then*, and *finally*.

V L S M B P I N

INTERPERSONAL

I Like to...

Describe something that you like to do that follows an order. Be sure to use transitional words like *first*, *second*, *next*, *then*, and *finally* to describe the sequence.

Share your description with a friend. What do you like best about your partner's description? What questions do you have about your partner's description? What suggestion(s) do you have to improve it?

V L S M B P I N

UNDERSTANDING

Author's Organization

Why did the author choose to use a sequence to organize the information in the reading?

V L S M B P I N

SELF-EXPRESSIVE

Act Out

Act out the steps described in the piece you read. See if your partner can figure out what the topic is. (If you've both read the same piece, then take turns acting out each step.)

V L S M B P I N

This Task Rotation can help you meet these K-5 standards…

> R.CCR: 1, 3, 8*, 10 *esp. RI.3.8*
> W.CCR: 1, 4, 10
> SL.CCR: 5
> L.CCR: 1, 2

COMMON CORE CORNER

NONFICTION: COMPARISON

Sometimes an author compares and contrasts two things or ideas. Read a piece of nonfiction that compares and contrasts two things or ideas. Make sure you complete the activities in order.

A

B

MASTERY

Criteria for Comparison

1. What are the two things or ideas the author is comparing?

A. _____

and

B. _____

What criteria (size, shape, use, etc.) does the author use to compare these two things or ideas?

V **L** S M B P I N

INTERPERSONAL

Be a Critic

4. Do you feel the two things or ideas are more alike or more different? Write a paragraph (or more) explaining your opinion. Be sure to write an interesting first sentence and a solid conclusion.

V **L** S M B P I N

UNDERSTANDING

Compare & Contrast

2. How are these two things or ideas similar? How are they different?

A. _____	B. _____

Similarities

V **L** **S** M B P I N

SELF-EXPRESSIVE

Flip Book

3. Make a flip book with words and pictures to explain the differences between the two things or ideas you read about.

Example: a frog and a toad

A frog…	A frog…	A frog…	A frog…
but a toad…	and a toad…	while a toad…	however, a toad…

V **L** **S** M B P I N

COMMON CORE CORNER

This Task Rotation can help you meet these K-5 standards…

> R.CCR: 1, 8, 10
> W.CCR: 1, 4, 9, 10
> SL.CCR: NA
> L.CCR: 1, 2, 5* *esp. L.4-5.5a*

NONFICTION: ARGUMENT

Sometimes an author makes an argument and provides reasons and evidence to support the argument. Read a piece of nonfiction in which the author makes an argument.

MASTERY

What's the Argument?

What is the author's argument? What claim is he or she making?

V L S M B P I N

INTERPERSONAL

What Do You Think?

What is your opinion about the author's argument? Do you agree or disagree with the argument? What reasons can you provide to support your opinion?

V L S M B P I N

UNDERSTANDING

What Are the Reasons?

What evidence or reasons does the author include to support the argument?

V L S M B P I N

SELF-EXPRESSIVE

Say It With a Simile

An argument without reasons is like…

- A car without fuel.
- A table without legs.
- A plant without water.

Pick one and explain.

V L S M B P I N

This Task Rotation can help you meet these K-5 standards...

> R.CCR: 1, 2, 7, 9, 10
> W.CCR: 3, 7, 8, 9
> SL.CCR: NA
> L.CCR: 1, 2, 6

COMMON CORE CORNER

LET'S GO... RESEARCH!

Select a topic that interests you. Find at least two sources to help you research your topic. Use the activities below to organize, develop, and reflect on the research project.

Topic: _____

Sources: _____

MASTERY

Know Your Topic

1. Make a list of what you know about the topic as well as what you would like to know. As you conduct your research, keep track of new information you learn.

Know	Would Like to Know	Learned

V L **S** M B **P** I N

INTERPERSONAL

Reflecting on Your Research

4. Write a letter to a friend telling him or her about the interesting things you learned from researching your topic and how you conducted your research.

V L S M B **P** I N

UNDERSTANDING

Topic Web

2. Organize the information you learned about your topic into a web showing the topic, subtopics, and details.

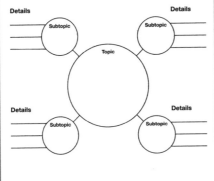

V **L** **S** M B **P** I N

SELF-EXPRESSIVE

Acrostic

3. Create an acrostic for your topic. Write out the name of your topic down the page. Then, for each letter in your topic, use meaningful information that you learned from your research to explain your topic.

Example: cats

C *lean themselves with their rough tongues*

A *re mammals—give live birth, have fur, are warm-blooded*

T *ake naps throughout the day*

S *talk and hunt other animals like mice, lizards, and birds*

V L S M B **P** I N

Poetry

Task Rotations

While we encourage you to use the following Task Rotations in your classroom, they are meant to be something more than reproducibles. We like to think of them as models, ideas, inspiration—as "mind starters" you can use and modify to meet the needs of your students while sparking their passion to read.

Note: Full-size copies of select Task Rotations from this genre are available for download from the Reading Style Resource Center at www.ThoughtfulClassroom.com/ReadingResources.

This Task Rotation can help you meet these K-5 standards... > R.CCR: 4, 5*, 10 *esp. RL.K.5, RL.4.5* > W.CCR: 10 > SL.CCR: 5 > L.CCR: 1, 2, 5* *esp. L.4-5.5a*

WHAT IS A POEM?

Poems use words, sounds, and rhythm to express feelings and create pictures in our mind. Some poems rhyme, some do not. Poets want their readers to feel a certain way and to imagine and "see" the ideas presented in their poems. Select a poem to read. Then respond to the activities below.

MASTERY

Picture a Poem

What is the poem about? Use words and a picture to describe it.

V L S M B P I N

INTERPERSONAL

Poetry Emotion

What are the feelings the poem is trying to express?

V L S M B P I N

UNDERSTANDING

Poetry vs. Writing

How is a poem different from other types of writing?

V L S M B P I N

SELF-EXPRESSIVE

Poetry as Music

How is a poem like a song?

V L S M B P I N

COMMON CORE CORNER

This Task Rotation can help you meet these K-5 standards...

> R.CCR: 4*, 10 *esp. RL.1-2.4*   > SL.CCR: NA
> W.CCR: 1, 4, 10   > L.CCR: 1, 2, 3, 5

RHYME TIME!

Sometimes rhyming words are used in poetry to help express feelings. Read or listen to a poem that uses rhyming words. Then respond to the activities below.

MASTERY

Word Search

Circle (or write) the words in the poem that rhyme.

V L S M B P I N

INTERPERSONAL

Now, With Feeling

Describe how a rhyming poem makes you feel.

V L S M B P I N

UNDERSTANDING

Poem vs. Poem

Why might a poet choose to use rhyming words in a poem?

V L S M B P I N

SELF-EXPRESSIVE

Favorites

Pick a favorite thing (food, season, sport, type of music, place, etc.). Write three or four words that help you picture your favorite thing. Then use these words to create a *rhyming poem* about your favorite thing.

V L S M B P I N

This Task Rotation can help you meet these K-5 standards...

> R.CCR: 4, 10
> W.CCR: 1, 2, 4, 10
> SL.CCR: NA
> L.CCR: 1, 2, 3, 5

COMMON CORE CORNER

NOT ALL POEMS RHYME

Sometimes a poem doesn't use rhyming words. Instead it uses descriptive words to express an idea or feeling. Read or listen to a non-rhyming poem. Then respond to the activities below.

MASTERY

INTERPERSONAL

Word Search

Circle (or write) the words in the poem that help you see the ideas or sense the feelings.

V L S M B P I N

Pick Your Poetry

Do you prefer rhyming poems or non-rhyming poems? Why?

V L S M B P I N

UNDERSTANDING

SELF-EXPRESSIVE

Poem vs. Poem

In your own words, explain how a non-rhyming poem is different from a rhyming poem.

V L S M B P I N

Favorites

Pick a favorite thing (food, season, sport, type of music, place, etc.). Write three or four words that help you picture your favorite thing. Then use these words to create a *non-rhyming poem* about your favorite thing.

V L S M B P I N

COMMON CORE CORNER

This Task Rotation can help you meet these K-5 standards...

> R.CCR: 1, 4*, 10 *esp. RL.1.4* > SL.CCR: 5
> W.CCR: 1, 10 > L.CCR: 1, 2, 5

GET THE PICTURE?

Poets use descriptive language to help the reader see what the poem is about. We call this descriptive language *imagery*. Read or listen to a poem. Then complete the activities below in the proper order to help you better understand how poets use imagery to make their poems come to life.

MASTERY

1. Collect words and phrases from the poem that help you create images in your mind.

V L S M B P I N

INTERPERSONAL

2. What is your favorite image in the poem? Why is it your favorite?

V L S M B P I N

UNDERSTANDING

4. *All readers see the same images when they read a poem.* Do you agree or disagree? Explain your answer.

V L S M B P I N

SELF-EXPRESSIVE

3. Draw what you see in your mind. Below your drawing, write the words from the poem that helped you see the image. Share your drawing and words with a friend.

V L S M B P I N

This Task Rotation can help you meet these K-5 standards…

> R.CCR: 5, 9, 10 > SL.CCR: NA
> W.CCR: 1, 10 > L.CCR: 1, 2

COMMON CORE CORNER

POTPOURRI OF POETRY

Poetry comes in all different styles. Some poetry is connected to specific cultures and can have a specific number of beats or lines. Try to think of all the different types of poems you have read or heard of, and then respond to the activities below.

MASTERY

Types of Poetry

Can you name four different types of poems? List them below. Then, tell what you know about each type.

1.

2.

3.

4.

V   L   S   M   B   P   I   N

INTERPERSONAL

Pick Your Poem

Select your favorite type of poem and tell why it is your favorite.

V   L   S   M   B   P   I   N

UNDERSTANDING

Analyzing Poetry

Pick two types of poems and explain how they are similar and different.

A. _____	B. _____

Similarities

V   L   S   M   B   P   I   N

SELF-EXPRESSIVE

Be a Poet

Create a new poem of your favorite type.

V   L   S   M   B   P   I   N

Designing
Task Rotations
for Your
Classroom

So far in this book we've presented a variety of Task Rotations applicable for use with a wide range of fiction, nonfiction, and poetry texts. In this section, you'll learn a simple, step-by-step process for designing your own Task Rotations to help you meet the demands of the specific texts your students read and the standards you address in your classroom.

To design a Task Rotation, follow these six steps:

Steps in Designing a Task Rotation

1. Select your text and standards.

2. Establish student-friendly learning targets.

3. Design four style-based tasks aligned with your targets.

4. Develop assessment criteria for each task.

5. Create an engaging hook to capture student interest and activate background knowledge.

6. Establish a work plan outlining what you and your students need to do before, during, and after the Task Rotation.

To see how this process works, let's follow a fourth-grade teacher as he develops a Task Rotation on argument using a recent article for elementary readers on the potential dangers of owning an exotic pet. His completed Task Rotation appears in Figure 10 (p. 73).

Figure 10: Teacher's Task Rotation – Exotic Pets: Should People Own Them?

MASTERY

The article we just read gives us reasons why exotic animals can be good pets and bad pets. Use the organizer below to collect reasons for each side of the argument.

Exotic Animals Are Good Pets Because...	Exotic Animals Are Bad Pets Because...
1.	1.
2.	2.
3.	3.

INTERPERSONAL

Your friend is thinking about getting an exotic animal as a pet. Help your friend make an informed decision. What advice would you give your friend? Why would you give this advice?

My Advice to a Friend...
My Reasoning...

UNDERSTANDING

What kind of pet do you have? Compare your pet to an exotic pet. How are they alike? How are they different? Give two ways they are similar and two ways they are different. If you don't have a pet of your own, pick a traditional pet (like a cat, dog, fish, or bird) to compare to an exotic pet.

My Pet	Exotic Pet
1.	1.
2.	2.

Similarities
1.
2.

SELF-EXPRESSIVE

No matter what your feelings are about exotic pets, they're not going anywhere. Some people will still keep exotic pets. Based on what you've learned, create a chart that gives people three guidelines for safely keeping an exotic pet. For each guideline, create a visual to help owners remember the guideline and the reasons behind each guideline.

	Guideline	Visual	Reasoning
1.			
2.			
3.			

Now let's look at how this teacher used the planning process and forms to develop his Task Rotation.

Sample Planning Form: How One Teacher Developed a Task Rotation

1. Select your text and standards.

What text (or information source) will you use?

I've selected a kid-friendly article about the potential issues with exotic pet ownership.

Why did you select this text? What standards will it help you address?

We've been looking at arguments recently, but so far the readings have presented mainly one argument. What I like about this reading is it presents two equally compelling arguments—one for and one against owning exotic pets. So, I'll be able to take student thinking to the next level by asking, How do you decide which argument is best? This focus on argument will help students meet these Common Core State Standards:

- RI.4.2 — Determine the main idea of a text and explain how it is supported by key details; summarize the text.
- RI.4.8 — Explain how an author uses reasons and evidence to support particular points in a text.
- W.4.1 — Write opinion pieces on topics or texts, supporting a point of view with reasons and information.

2. Establish student-friendly learning targets.

What are your student-friendly learning targets?

- I can identify an argument in a reading.
- I can state both sides of an argument and explain the reasoning behind each.
- I can explain how evidence makes an argument more persuasive.
- I can use words and pictures to make an argument of my own.

[Note that the teacher has written his targets as "I can" statements.]

3. Design four style-based tasks aligned with your targets.

[Note: The full Task Rotation appears in Figure 10 on page 73.]

MASTERY

The article we just read gives us reasons why exotic animals can be good pets and bad pets. Use an organizer to collect reasons for each side of the argument.

INTERPERSONAL

Your friend is thinking about getting an exotic animal as a pet. Help your friend make an informed decision. What advice would you give your friend? Why would you give this advice?

UNDERSTANDING

What kind of pet do you have? Compare your pet to an exotic pet. How are they alike? How are they different? Give two ways they are similar and two ways they are different. If you don't have a pet of your own, pick a traditional pet (like a cat, dog, fish, or bird) to compare to an exotic pet.

SELF-EXPRESSIVE

No matter what your feelings are about exotic pets, they're not going anywhere. Some people will still keep exotic pets. Based on what you've learned, create a chart that gives people three guidelines for safely keeping an exotic pet. For each guideline, create a visual to help owners remember the guideline and the reasons behind each guideline.

4. Develop assessment criteria for each task.

	What are your assessment criteria?
Mastery Task	Can the student restate both sides of the argument?
Understanding Task	Can the student identify key similarities and differences between an exotic pet and a traditional pet?
Self-Expressive Task	Can the student develop three guidelines for exotic pet ownership? Do the images capture the essence of each guideline? Do the reasons explain the importance or relevance of each guideline?
Interpersonal Task	Can the student make a personal and persuasive argument?

5. *Create an engaging hook to capture student interest and activate background knowledge.*

What is your hook—how will you engage students?

I'll draw students in by asking them to think about their personal experiences with arguments and making good decisions. I'll pose these questions, give students time to discuss their ideas with a partner, and then have them share with the class:

- How many of you have had an argument? Have you ever experienced an argument in which both sides seem to have good points?
- Now think about this question: How do you make a good decision when both sides seem to have good points?

What is your bridge—how will you connect students' responses from the hook to the lesson?

I'll connect students' thinking from the hook to the article in this way:

- So far we have looked at how an author makes one good argument. Now we're going to look at how two good but opposite arguments can be made about the same topic. And our topic today is exotic pets. Let's talk a little bit about what an exotic pet is before we begin reading our article.

6. Establish a work plan outlining what you and your students need to do before, during, and after the Task Rotation.

<table>
<tr><td rowspan="2">BEFORE</td><td>Are my students familiar with style? If not, how will I introduce style?</td><td>My students are familiar with the four styles and the process. As a reminder, I'll refer them to the Task Rotation poster in our classroom.</td></tr>
<tr><td>How will I "hook" students' attention and introduce the lesson?</td><td>I'll pose two questions about experiencing an argument and making good decisions and have students share their ideas. Then students will consider whether they'd like to own an exotic pet and whether that's a good idea before reading the article.</td></tr>
<tr><td rowspan="7">DURING</td><td>Will students complete all of the tasks or will they choose some?</td><td>This time students will complete all four tasks.</td></tr>
<tr><td>In what order will students work on the activities?</td><td>I will have students work in this order: Mastery, Understanding, Interpersonal, and close with Self-Expressive.</td></tr>
<tr><td>Will students work together or individually?</td><td>Students will complete the first three tasks by themselves. For the final Self-Expressive task I'll pair students up.</td></tr>
<tr><td>Is any modeling needed?</td><td>Yes. For the Self-Expressive task I'll model how I would develop a guideline, icon, and reasons using a different topic, like "guidelines for classroom behavior."</td></tr>
<tr><td>What resources will students need?</td><td>Students need the article to read and paper to write and draw on.</td></tr>
<tr><td>How will I formatively assess student progress?</td><td>While students are working, I'll circulate around the room to make sure each student is on track and give feedback as needed. For the last task, I'll visit with each pair to make sure students are collaborating effectively.</td></tr>
<tr><td rowspan="1"></td><td></td></tr>
<tr><td>AFTER</td><td>How will I encourage reflection and discussion?</td><td>I'll ask students to discuss the activities that helped them the most and which ones were the most challenging.

I'll also ask students to do a simple reflection that goes like this:
• Before reading the article I thought... Now I think...</td></tr>
</table>

Blank Planning Forms

Use the forms on the next few pages to plan and develop your own
Task Rotations for your classroom. You can make copies of these forms
or access these forms online from our Reading Style Resource Center
at www.ThoughtfulClassroom.com/ReadingResources.

1. Select your text and standards.

What text (or information source) will you use?

Why did you select this text? What standards will it help you address?

2. Establish student-friendly learning targets.

What are your student-friendly learning targets?

3. Design four style-based tasks aligned with your targets.

Mastery

Understanding

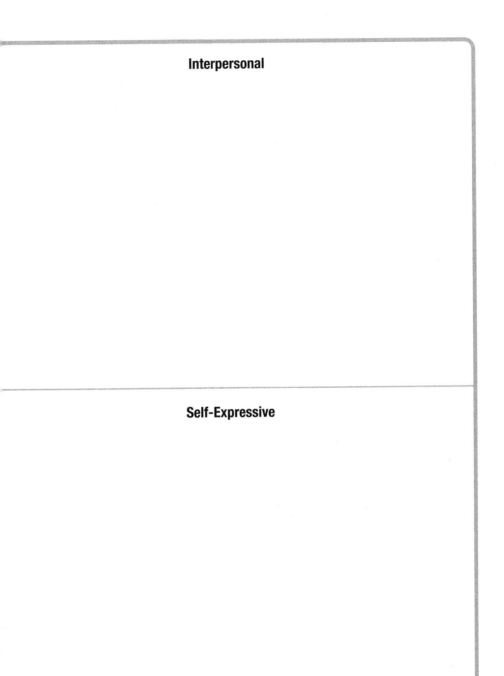

Interpersonal

Self-Expressive

4. Develop assessment criteria for each task.

What are your assessment criteria?
Mastery Task
Understanding Task
Self-Expressive Task
Interpersonal Task

5. Create an engaging hook to capture student interest and activate background knowledge.

What is your hook—how will you engage students?

What is your bridge—how will you connect students' responses from the hook to the lesson?

6. Establish a work plan outlining what you and your students need to do before, during, and after the Task Rotation.

BEFORE	Are my students familiar with style? If not, how will I introduce style?	
	How will I "hook" students' attention and introduce the lesson?	
DURING	Will students complete all of the tasks or will they choose some?	
	In what order will students work on the activities?	
	Will students work together or individually?	
	Is any modeling needed?	
	What resources will students need?	
	How will I formatively assess student progress?	
AFTER	How will I encourage reflection and discussion?	

Planning and Implementation Notes

References

Carrozza, C. (1996). Using learning styles and multiple intelligences to differentiate instruction and assessment. In R. W. Strong & H. F. Silver, *An introduction to thoughtful curriculum and assessment* (pp. 145-152). Woodbridge, NJ: Thoughtful Education Press.

Common Core State Standards Initiative. (n.d.). *Common core state standards for English language arts & literacy in history/social studies, science, and technical subjects*. Available: http://www.corestandards.org/the-standards/english-language-arts-standards.

Gardner, H. (1999). *Intelligence reframed: Multiple intelligences for the 21st century.* New York: Basic Books.

Gardner, H. (2011). *Frames of mind: The theory of multiple intelligences (3rd edition)*. New York: Basic Books. First edition published 1983.

Gregory, G. (2005). *Differentiating instruction with style: Aligning teacher and learner intelligences for maximum achievement*. Thousand Oaks, CA: Corwin Press.

Jung, C. G. (1923). *Psychological types*. Trans. H. G. Baynes. New York: Harcourt, Brace & Company.

Kise, J. A. G. (2007). *Differentiation through personality types: A framework for instruction, assessment, and classroom management*. Thousand Oaks, CA: Corwin Press.

Mamchur, C. (1996). *A teacher's guide to cognitive type theory and learning style*. Alexandria, VA: ASCD.

McCarthy, B. (1982). *The 4mat system*. Arlington Heights, IL: Excel Publishing.

Myers, I. B. (1962). *The Myers-Briggs Type Indicator*. Palo Alto, CA: Consulting Psychologists Press.

Myers, I. B., McCaulley, M. H., Quenk, N. L., & Hammer, A. L. (1998). *MBTI manual: A guide to the development and use of the Myers-Briggs Type Indicator (3rd edition).* Palo Alto, CA: Consulting Psychologists Press.

Pajak, E. (2003). *Honoring diverse teaching styles: A guide for supervisors.* Alexandria, VA: ASCD.

Payne, D. & VanSant, S. (2009). *Great minds don't think alike: Success for students through the application of psychological type in schools.* Gainesville, FL. Center for the Applications of Psychological Type.

Silver, H. F. & Hanson, J. R. (1998). *Learning styles and strategies (3rd edition).* Woodbridge, NJ: Thoughtful Education Press.

Silver, H. F., Jackson, J. W., & Moirao, D. R. (2011). *Task rotation: Strategies for differentiating activities and assessments by learning style.* Alexandria, VA: ASCD.

Silver, H. F. & Strong, R. W. (2004). *Learning style inventory for students.* Ho-Ho-Kus, NJ: Thoughtful Education Press.

Sternberg, R. J. (2006). Recognizing neglected strengths. *Educational Leadership*, 64 (1), 30-35.

Strong, R. W., Silver, H. F. & Perini, M. J. (2008). *Reading for academic success, grades 2-6: Differentiated strategies for struggling, average, and advanced readers.* Thousand Oaks, CA: Corwin Press.

Thoughtful Education Press (2007). *Questioning styles and strategies: How to use questions to engage and motivate different styles of learners.* Ho-Ho-Kus, NJ: Author.